NORTH DAKOTA

by E. Hoover Severin

GARETH**STEVENS**

P U B L I S H I N G

A Member of the WRC Media Family of Companies

Please visit our web site at: www.garethstevens.com
For a free color catalog describing Gareth Stevens Publishing's
list of high-quality books and multimedia programs, call
1-800-542-2595 (USA) or 1-800-387-3178 (Canada).
Gareth Stevens Publishing's fax: (877) 542-2596.

Library of Congress Cataloging-in-Publication Data

Severin, E. Hoover.
    North Dakota / E. Hoover Severin.
      p. cm. — (Portraits of the states)
    Includes bibliographical references and index.
    ISBN-10: 0-8368-4706-7   ISBN-13: 978-0-8368-4706-2 (lib. bdg.)
    ISBN-10: 0-8368-4723-7   ISBN-13: 978-0-8368-4723-9 (softcover)
    1. North Dakota—Juvenile literature. I. Title. II. Series.
    F636.3.S48   2007
    978.4—dc22   2005036639

This edition first published in 2007 by
Gareth Stevens Publishing
A Weekly Reader Company
1 Reader's Digest Rd.
Pleasantville, NY 10570-7000 USA

This edition copyright © 2007 by Gareth Stevens, Inc.

Editorial direction: Mark J. Sachner
Project manager: Jonatha A. Brown
Editor: Catherine Gardner
Art direction and design: Tammy West
Picture research: Diane Laska-Swanke
Indexer: Walter Kronenberg
Production: Jessica Morris and Robert Kraus

Picture credits: Cover, pp. 4, 12, 22, 24, 26, 27 © John Elk III; p. 5 U.S. Fish &
Wildlife Service; pp. 6, 8 © MPI/Getty Images; pp. 9, 11 © North Wind Picture
Archives; pp. 15, 16, 18, 21 © Tom Bean; p. 17 © CORBIS; p. 25 © AP Images;
p. 28 © State Historical Society of North Dakota 0262-03; p. 29 © Robert W.
Kelley/Time & Life Pictures/Getty Images

Printed in the United States of America

2 3 4 5 6 7 8 9 10 09 08 07

CONTENTS

Words that are defined in the Glossary appear
in **bold** the first time they are used in the text.

On the Cover: North Dakota's badlands are rugged and beautiful.
The badlands lie in the western part of the state.

Introduction

Welcome to North Dakota. This great state is packed with adventure and fun! You can see Native American dances. You can watch shaggy buffalo roaming the grasslands. You can visit a museum to see huge dinosaur bones.

North Dakota is also home to the Badlands. Here, colorful **canyons** and cliffs break up the land. Some people say the Badlands look like a scene from a different planet!

This state has freezing cold winters and hot summers. In winter, you can go ice fishing and ice skating. In summer, you can attend fairs and festivals. At any time of year, you are sure to have a good time in North Dakota.

These tall rock towers are called hoodoos. You can see them in the Badlands of North Dakota.

The state flag of North Dakota.

NORTH DAKOTA FACTS

- Became the 39th U.S. State: November 2, 1889
- Population (2006): 635,867
- Capital: Bismarck
- Biggest Cities: Fargo, Bismarck, Grand Forks
- Size: 70,665 square miles (183,022 square kilometers)
- Nickname: The Peace Garden State
- State Tree: American elm
- State Flower: Wild prairie rose
- State Grass: Western wheatgrass
- State Bird: Western meadowlark

History

Thousands of years ago, Native Americans lived in the place we now call North Dakota. They hunted buffalo and other large animals. Much later, Native people began to plant crops.

White Explorers

In 1682, the French claimed most of the land in the middle of North America. Some of the land they claimed was in North Dakota. The Spanish wanted this land, too. For many years, one country and then the other took control.

The Mandan people made homes of wooden poles covered with mud and buffalo hides.

In 1738, a white man visited the area for the first time. Pierre Gaultier de Varennes de La Vérendrye was a French fur trader. He came from Canada and went about as far as what is now Bismarck. He met at least one group of Natives on his trip. These people were Mandans.

In 1803, the United States bought a huge piece

of land from France. This was the Louisiana Purchase. Half of North Dakota was included in the sale.

Americans soon began to explore the area. The first of them were Meriwether Lewis and William Clark. They tried to follow rivers across the country. Their group headed up the Missouri River to North Dakota. They spent one winter there and then kept going west.

For some time, the British claimed the other half of North Dakota. They built a trading post in Pembina in 1812. It was the first lasting white settlement in what is now North Dakota. Six years later, Britain gave up all of this land to the United States.

The Dakota Territory

In 1861, the U.S. Congress set up the Dakota **Territory**. It was far from the more settled lands. Most white people were afraid of attacks by Natives. Travel was slow

Famous People of North Dakota

Sacagawea

Born: About 1786, near Salmon, Idaho

Died: unknown

Sacagawea was a Native of the Shoshone tribe. She met Lewis and Clark in North Dakota. She became a guide for their group. Her husband and baby went with them. Sacagawea found plants for the explorers to eat. She also helped them talk to other Natives. She was the only woman on the trip. She worked hard to make it a success.

IN NORTH DAKOTA'S HISTORY

Bringing Sickness

When white people came to this area, they brought buttons, tools, and other gifts for the Natives. But not all of the things they brought were good. The whites also brought sickness. Many Natives died from diseases brought by whites. In 1837, **smallpox** killed most of the Mandan and Hidatsa people.

and difficult, too. At first, few people settled there.

The U.S. government sent soldiers to the new territory. They chased the Sioux and fought with them. The fighting went on for years. In the end, the Army won. Then, in 1882, most of the Natives were sent to **reservations** to live.

The Homestead Act

In 1862, the U.S. Congress passed the Homestead Act. This law gave free land to

white settlers who would move to the West. Many people wanted free land. Some of them came to North Dakota to settle.

Many homesteaders built homes in the Red River Valley.

The settlers found that life was difficult here. Winters were icy cold, and summers were hot and dry. Lightning started grass fires, and swarms of grasshoppers sometimes ate the crops.

Growth

The first railroad was built in North Dakota in the 1870s and early 1880s.

FUN FACTS

Sod Houses

Few trees grew in this area. Settlers could not build their houses from wood. Instead, they used blocks of soil and roots. These blocks are known as sod. The settlers stacked up chunks of sod to make the walls of their homes. These houses were called "soddies."

Towns grew up along the railroad line. The people of the Dakota Territory now had stores and banks. Trains brought supplies, newspapers, and mail.

North Dakota became a U.S. state in 1889. By then, many big wheat farms had been built. Some farmers grew rich. News of their success drew more people to the state. Settlers came from other states and countries to farm. Big companies from the East began buying huge areas of land. The number of people in the state doubled in the years from 1890 to 1910.

Hard Times

In 1890, the price of wheat fell. Farmers lost money. Some settlers had to leave their homesteads.

Cattle ranchers had a hard

IN NORTH DAKOTA'S HISTORY

Killing the Buffalo

In the late 1800s, white hunters began killing buffalo from trains. They shot at the buffalo from the train windows and left the dead animals on the ground. Soon, most of the buffalo in North Dakota were gone. This was a great loss for the Native Americans who lived there. They lost their source of food and clothing. The Natives were forced to try to find a new way to survive.

time, too. Large companies had brought cattle into the Badlands. The cattle died in the summer because they had no water, and they froze to death in the winter.

In the early 1900s, the farmers and ranchers still struggled. They worked together to help themselves, but they had a hard time. They could not control prices or the weather.

In 1929, the **Great**

Depression began. All over the country, businesses closed, and people lost their jobs. North Dakota had even more problems than most states. A very bad **drought** hit the state in 1936. Little rain fell, so crops dried up and died. Some people left the state to find work in other places.

Better Times

In the 1930s, the U.S. government started programs that made new jobs. Workers in North Dakota built bridges and roads. They dug big ditches, too. Soon, the ditches began to carry water from rivers to farmers' fields.

In 1941, the United States entered World War II. The price of wheat went up. North Dakota farmers helped feed the soldiers during the war.

In the late 1800s, men worked through a long, cold winter to lay railroad track near Bismarck.

The war ended in 1945. Two years later, workers began building a big dam on the Missouri River. The Garrison Dam took seven years to build. This project created many jobs. Then, oil was found near Tioga in 1951. Soon, the oil fields created jobs for people, too.

This power plant was built at the Garrison Dam. It uses the water from the Missouri River to make electric power.

North Dakota Today

Today, North Dakota has clean lakes and rivers. The air is fresh, and the people are friendly. This state is a peaceful place to live or to visit.

FUN FACTS

Famous Name For a Lake

After the Garrison Dam was built, a lake formed behind it. It is Lake Sakakawea. This lake is good for fishing and water sports. It has helped bring **tourists** to the state. It was named for Sacagawea, the Native American woman who guided Lewis and Clark. Her name is spelled in many different ways.

Time Line

1682	France claims most of the land now in North Dakota.
1803	France sells part of North Dakota to the United States in the Louisiana Purchase.
1818	Britain gives up the rest of North Dakota to the United States.
1861	The U.S. Congress sets up the Dakota Territory.
1862	The Homestead Act is passed; this opens land in North Dakota to white settlement.
1881	The first railroad across North Dakota is finished.
1882	Native people in North Dakota are forced to move to reservations.
1889	North Dakota becomes a U.S. state on November 2.
1890–1910	The number of white people living in North Dakota more than doubles.
1930s	North Dakota suffers through the Great Depression and a long drought.
1951	Oil is discovered in North Dakota.
1954	The Garrison Dam is finished; Lake Sakakawea begins to form behind it.
1966	The state is hit by the most severe blizzard in its history.
1997	Floods damage property in the Red River Valley.

People

Northorth Dakota is a good-sized state, but it has a small **population**. Only two other states in the country have fewer people than North Dakota.

About six out of every ten people in North Dakota live in or near cities. The rest of the people in the state live on farms and ranches and in small towns. Fargo is the biggest city in the state. Bismarck and Grand Forks are next in size. None of these cities is very big.

Hispanics
This chart shows the different racial backgrounds of people in North Dakota. In the 2000 U.S. Census, 1.2 percent of the people in North Dakota called themselves Latino or Hispanic. Most of them or their relatives came from places where Spanish is spoken. Hispanics do not appear on this chart because they may come from any racial background.

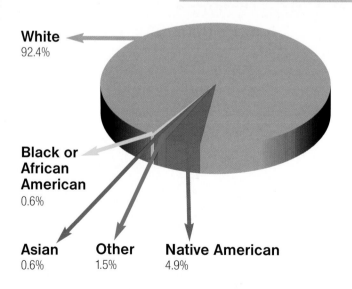

The People of North Dakota

Total Population 635,867

White
92.4%

Black or
African
American
0.6%

Asian
0.6%

Other
1.5%

Native American
4.9%

Percentages are based on the 2000 Census.

The People of the Past

Many towns in North Dakota hold "Crazy Days" to celebrate their history and attract tourists.

The Homestead Act of 1862 offered free land to settlers who agreed to live on the land for five years. This offer brought many settlers to North Dakota. Some of them were Americans, but most were from Germany and Norway. Settlers came from other parts of Europe and from Canada, too.

By 1910, more than 70 percent of the people who lived in the state were **immigrants**. No other state had such a high percentage of people who came from other countries.

People from the same country often settled near each other. They brought songs and dances from their old lands. Today, some of the towns still hold festivals that were brought to the state by the early settlers.

Native Americans celebrate their history and way of life at festivals around the state. They get together to dance, sing, and hold meetings.

Less than 5 percent of the people who live in North Dakota today are Native Americans. More than half of all Natives in the state live on reservations. Many Natives earn less than most other people in the state. They often have trouble finding work and supporting their families.

The People Today

Most of the people who live in North Dakota today were born in the United States. Many can trace their families back to the early Norwegian and German settlers.

Today, few people move here from other parts of the world. Most of them come from places such as Canada, India, and Cuba.

Education and Religion

In its early days, North Dakota did not have any schools. Some children were taught by their parents. Other children were taught in their own homes by teachers who went from place to place. The first school opened in Pembina in 1818. Public schools were not set up in North Dakota until 1862.

The University of North Dakota was the state's first university. It opened in Grand Forks in 1883. Today, the state has many colleges and universities.

Most people in this state are Christian. More than half of these people are Catholic and Lutheran. Some Jews and people of other faiths live here, too.

Famous People of North Dakota

Carl Ben Eielson

Born: July 20, 1897, Hatton, North Dakota

Died: November 9, 1929, off the coast of Alaska

Carl Ben Eielson was the first person to fly over the Arctic Ocean. He tried to cross the North Pole for the first time in 1927. He had engine trouble and had to land his plane on floating ice. Then, he and his partner started walking. They walked through the Arctic for twelve days. The two men covered 125 miles (201 km) on foot before they finally reached safety! In 1928, they tried again. This time, Eielson succeeded. He flew all the way over the North Pole to Norway. He died in a plane crash the next year.

The Land

The state of North Dakota is in the northern United States. It is shaped like a rectangle. The right side of this rectangle is ragged. There, the Red River of the North forms the eastern border of the state.

A Valley, Prairie, and Plains

The Red River of the North flows through a big flat **valley**. In some places, this valley is 40 miles (64 km) wide. Most of the land in the valley is used for farming. This is some of the best farmland in the world. Wild grasses can still be seen here and there. These grasses can grow taller than a person.

FUN FACTS

Shaping the Land

Most of the hills and valleys of North Dakota were formed thousands of years ago. At that time, huge, thick sheets of ice covered the land. These sheets of ice were **glaciers**. Later, the glaciers melted and left big piles of gravel and dirt behind. These big piles became grass-covered hills.

Buffalo herds now live in large parks around the state. Here a large herd roams safe from harm.

NORTH DAKOTA

West of the valley, the **prairie** begins. This land is higher, and it slopes upward to the west. The prairie is made up of rolling hills and is dotted with lakes and ponds. Some of the ponds dry up during the summer.

Many kinds of grasses grow here. In the east, the grasses grow tall, and in the west, they are quite short.

The highest land is found in the southwestern part of the state. This area is in a huge natural region called the Great Plains. The plains are hilly here. Some hills have steep sides. They are called **buttes**. The highest point in the state is White Butte. It rises 3,506 feet (1,069 meters).

Rivers and Lakes

The state has many rivers and lakes. The two longest rivers are the Missouri River and the Red River of the North. The largest lake is Lake Sakakawea. This lake was created when the Garrison Dam was built on the Missouri River. Devils Lake is the biggest natural lake in the state.

Major Rivers

Missouri River
2,466 miles (3,968 km) long

Red River of the North
355 miles (571 km) long

Sheyenne River
325 miles (525 km) long

Climate

North Dakota has fierce weather. The winters bring snowy blizzards and freezing cold weather. Summers are very hot and dry. Strong winds often blow across the plains. Sometimes, little rain falls for months at a time. At other times,

FUN FACTS

The Badlands

The Badlands is a big, rocky valley in the south-western part of the state. Glaciers did not reach this area. Instead, water and wind carved many deep canyons and buttes. Elk, bighorn sheep, and wild horses roam among the cactuses and short grass. Snakes and coyotes can be found, too. This area got its name from the settlers who found that it was a bad place to travel through.

too much rain falls, and the rivers flood their banks.

Animals

The state's waterways and grasses offer homes to many birds. More ducks, geese, and other waterbirds nest in North Dakota than in almost any other state.

Tourists come to Lake Sakakawea to sail, fish, and enjoy water sports. This man-made lake is the largest lake in the state.

Golden eagles, sage hens, and hawks can also be seen.

White-tailed deer live all over the state. In the west, mule deer and antelope are common. Buffalo roam in parks and other protected places. Smaller animals include coyotes, squirrels, foxes, and rabbits. In the Badlands, prairie dogs build "dog towns" by digging tunnels under the ground.

5

Economy

In North Dakota, 90 percent of the land is used for farming and ranching. Wheat is the leading crop. In fact, only Kansas produces more wheat than this state does. North Dakota grows more sunflowers than any other U.S. state. Oats, barley, soybeans, rye, and sugar beets grow well here, too.

The state has many beef and dairy farms. Pigs, sheep, chickens, and turkeys are also raised on many farms.

Making Goods

Factories provide thousands of jobs for people in North Dakota. Some of the

A farmer cuts wheat on a large farm. Wheat is the biggest crop in North Dakota.

state's factory workers make farm equipment. Others make parts for airplanes and computers. Still others make cheese, grind flour, or package meat, such as steaks and sausages.

Natural Resources

Natural resources are things found in nature that can be used by people. Oil is the most important natural resource in North Dakota. Oil is used to make gasoline. Coal is very important, too. It is used to run electric power plants. North Dakota has more coal and electricity than its people need, so it sends some to other states. These states pay North Dakota for both its coal and electricity. Sand, clay, and gravel are mined here, too.

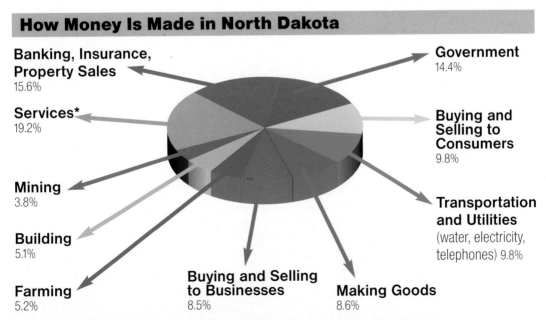

How Money Is Made in North Dakota

Banking, Insurance, Property Sales
15.6%

Services*
19.2%

Mining
3.8%

Building
5.1%

Farming
5.2%

Buying and Selling to Businesses
8.5%

Making Goods
8.6%

Government
14.4%

Buying and Selling to Consumers
9.8%

Transportation and Utilities
(water, electricity, telephones) 9.8%

* Services include jobs in hotels, restaurants, auto repair, medicine, teaching, and entertainment.

Government

Bismarck is the capital of North Dakota. The state's leaders work there. The government of this state has three parts. They are the executive, legislative, and judicial branches.

Executive Branch

The executive branch carries out the state's laws. The governor leads this branch. The lieutenant governor helps the governor. A team of people called the **cabinet** also works for the governor.

The capitol building is in Bismarck. It is one of the tallest capitols in the country. This building is nineteen stories high.

The members of the Legislative Assembly meet in this large hall. Here they make laws for the state of South Dakota.

Legislative Branch

The state legislature is called the Legislative Assembly. It has two parts. They are the Senate and the House of Representatives. These two groups work together to make laws for the state.

Judicial Branch

Judges and courts make up the judicial branch. Judges and courts may decide whether people who have been **accused of** committing crimes are guilty.

Local Government

North Dakota has fifty-three counties. Each county is run by a team of people. Most cities are run by a mayor and a city council.

NORTH DAKOTA'S STATE GOVERNMENT

Executive		Legislative		Judicial	
Office	**Length of Term**	**Body**	**Length of Term**	**Court**	**Length of Term**
Governor	4 years	Senate (47 members)	4 years	Supreme (5 justices)	10 years
Lieutenant Governor	4 years	House of Representatives (94 members)	4 years	District (42 judges)	6 years

Things to See and Do

North Dakota is full of fun things to see and do. It has many interesting museums, great parks, and fun festivals.

If you like dinosaurs, visit the Dakota Dinosaur Museum in Dickinson. It has fourteen full-size dinosaur models. It also has a huge skull and other bones.

Washburn is home to the Lewis and Clark Interpretive Center. Here, you can see canoes like the ones Lewis and Clark traveled in. You can also try on a buffalo robe. Fort Mandan is nearby. Lewis and Clark spent the winter of 1804 at this fort.

These huge dinosaur bones make an exciting display at the Dakota Dinosaur Museum in Dickinson.

In Jamestown, you can go to the National Buffalo Museum. It is home to a rare, all-white buffalo. Her name is White Cloud. Each July, the museum holds a birthday party for White Cloud. If you go to her party, you can eat birthday cake and watch a parade.

The Knife River Indian Villages National Historic Site is near Stanton. Here, you can visit an earth house and see how the Hidatsa once lived.

FUN FACTS

Strange Sights in the Badlands

Sometimes lightning strikes veins of coal in the Badlands. These lightning strikes start coal fires under the ground. Flames shoot into the air from cracks in the earth. At night, people can see the flames from miles away. Some of these fires cannot be put out. They have been burning for more than eighty years.

This house made of earth is part of the Knife Indian River Villages National Historic Site. Inside, you can see baskets and tools like those the Hidatsa once used.

Famous People of North Dakota

Era Bell Thompson

Born: August 10, 1905, Des Moines, Iowa

Died: December 30, 1986, Chicago, Illinois

Era Bell Thompson was African American. She and her family moved to North Dakota when she was five years old. Later, Thompson went to college in this state. She joined her school's track team. She was such a fast runner that she set speed records in some of her races.

When Thompson grew up, she became a famous writer. She worked on a magazine for black people and wrote books, too. One book told about her childhood in North Dakota. This book was *American Daughter*.

Parks

North Dakota has many places to enjoy nature. Theodore Roosevelt National Park is in the Badlands. It is a great place to camp and hike. Mule deer, elk, and wild horses live in the park.

Festivals and Powwows

Festivals offer fun for the whole family. Shiverfest is a winter festival at Devils Lake. Holes are cut in the ice so children can go ice fishing. They drop lines into the water and see who can catch the biggest fish. Snowmobiling and dogsled races also are part of this fun festival.

Powwows are good places to learn more about Native Americans. You can try Native foods and enjoy drumming, dancing, and crafts. Bismarck has one of the largest powwows in the state. It is held once a year in September.

Roger Maris makes a mighty swing during a game between the New York Yankees and the Detroit Tigers. Maris was one of the greatest home-run hitters of all time.

Famous People of North Dakota

Roger Eugene Maris

Born: September 10, 1934, Hibbing, Minnesota

Died: December 14, 1985, Houston, Texas

Roger Maris moved to Fargo when he was eight years old. As a boy, he liked sports. He played both football and baseball in high school. When he grew up, he became a professional baseball player with the New York Yankees. In 1961, Maris set a new record for hitting the most home runs during one season. He held that record for thirty-seven years.

accused of — blamed for

buttes — hills that have very steep sides and that often have flat tops

cabinet — people who help a political leader make decisions

canyons — deep, narrow valleys with steep sides and often with a river running through them

drought — a time when there is little rain and the land dries up

factories — buildings where goods are made

glaciers — large, very thick sheets of ice that cover the land

Great Depression — a time, in the 1930s, when many people lost jobs and businesses lost money

immigrants — people who leave one country to live in another country

population — the number of people who live in a place, such as a city, town, or state

powwows — a Native American gathering or ceremony

prairie — a large, grassy area of land

reservations — lands held aside by the government for a particular use

smallpox — a contagious disease like measles

territory — an area that belongs to a country

tourists — people who travel for fun

valley — an area of low ground between two hills

Books

If You Lived with the Sioux Indians. Ann McGovern (Rebound by Sagebrush)

Missouri River. Rivers of North America (series). Leon Gray (Gareth Stevens)

North Dakota. Rookie Read-About Geography (series). Pam Zollman (Children's Press)

P is for Peace Garden: A North Dakota Alphabet. Discover America State by State (series). Roxane Salonen (Sleeping Bear Press)

Sacagawea. Liselotte Erdrich (Carolrhoda Books)

Web Sites

Enchanted Learning: North Dakota
www.enchantedlearning.com/usa/states/northdakota/

I'm a Hero: Sacagawea
www.imahero.com/herohistory/sacagawea_herohistory.htm

North Dakota
www.worldalmanacforkids.com/explore/states/
northdakota.html

Theodore Roosevelt National Park
www.nps.gov/thro/

INDEX